A Mother's True Love

The power of life

Baljinder Kaur

MAPLE
PUBLISHERS

A Mother's True Love – The Power Of Life

Author: Baljinder Kaur

Copyright © Baljinder Kaur (2022)

The right of Baljinder Kaur to be identified as author of this work has been asserted by the author in accordance with section 77 and 78 of the Copyright, Designs and Patents Act 1988.

First Published in 2022

ISBN 978-1-915164-59-9 (Paperback)
978-1-915164-58-2 (E-Book)

Book cover design and Book layout by:
White Magic Studios
www.whitemagicstudios.co.uk

Published by:
Maple Publishers
1 Brunel Way,
Slough,
SL1 1FQ, UK
www.maplepublishers.com

This book I have written in the memory of my beautiful mother, who sadly passed away on the 2nd December 2002. I was so blessed to have had such a caring, talented and inspirational mum, not only was she my mum but the one person I could rely on no matter what, she was my best friend, my mum, and my world.

I had such a strong tight bond with my amazing mother, I felt like I lost parts of myself when I lost my mum. Anyone who has lost a special person will be able to relate to my pain.

It is okay to be lost, numb, shocked and disappointed to name a few. Everyone will feel differently and everyone will have to learn to deal with a loss in their own way. Personally I don't think time is a great healer and I feel as lost without my mum today as I did to begin with. All I can say is if you have a special mother who does so much for you, never take that for granted. I know not all mothers are the same, so whoever is that mother figure to you, cherish them, the one who is there for you no matter what.

My mum touched the hearts of so many people, she was such an amazing caring and beautiful person, even strangers benefited from her good heart. Not only did she come to the United Kingdom without speaking a word of English, she left behind all her family to start a new life with my dad. She went on to raise her children, do all the chores and run a very busy household, with guests always welcomed. She went on to working outside the family home as well.

My mum used to be a firm believer in "early to bed early to rise". She would wake up very early daily. Before all this social media, the 5am club was a trend!

I recall waking up to the scent of incense sticks burning and her cooking. Hearing the prayers was so comforting and the sense of peace. This has shaped me into a good routine myself.

Grief hurts beyond words because I miss my mum all the time and the impact has been hard on me, not a single day goes by without me thinking of you mum. Until we meet again I shall keep you close to my heart forever. Somedays I feel like I got this, I must accept you are at peace now and I know you are watching over me always and still guiding me, other days it still hurts like it's so fresh. Healing takes time but sometimes I don't think I will ever heal from the loss of my amazing mother.

My parents worked very hard and my mother was such a good role model to all.

> **LOOK OUT FOR THE PEOPLE WHO LOOK OUT FOR YOU. LOYALTY IS EVERYTHING.**

Life is full of so much variety of experiences - the good, the bad and some damn right awful. Whatever we go through we must accept one thing, that is very important and can help us avoid wasted time, that is we can only be accountable for our own behaviour and we can't be accountable for the behaviour of other adults around us.

How we react to others is all that we can control. Our inner peace is worth more than we may realise.

Growing up my mum use to always tell me to always count our blessings and appreciate everything in life, from the roof over our head to the shoes on my feet, she would say if we manage to eat food at least once a day we should be grateful, think of all the people around the world who have no home, praying for food and often have nothing but they can often be the people with the biggest hearts and are full of gratitude.

My mum would say that never take anything for granted, as in a single second everything can change. I was raised by a very special woman, who touched the hearts of so many people, those who knew her were blessed by her generosity, warm caring and loving heart.

That's why I question, when Covid 19 hit maybe it was to teach a lot of us a lesson on how much we may take for granted and how little we started to show gratitude for our daily blessings.

When I used to mention all the little quotes, advice and knowledge I've learnt from my mum to others they would comment on how lucky I was to have such an amazing mum and that I should write a book, so here it is and I hope it helps you as much as it has helped me become the strong person I am now.

To all those people who create their own stories of me in their heads and have always tried to stop me living my life, I'm no longer stoppable by your silly morals and like I was taught by my mum, remember we may be able to close the eyes of others but we can't close the eyes of the lord above us all.

I hope this book gives you lots of strength, encouragement and brings you the inner calm and the peace you deserve.

Never be afraid to put yourself on top of your to do list, self-care is essential and should always be on top of your agenda. Time spent on yourself isn't wasted time. Remember to get your priorities right. I'm talking about ensuring you get to keep your own mental well-being intact because 'if you don't look after yourself, who will?', as my mum would say to me.

You need to be in your children's present to be in their future, the bond won't just blossom if you aren't actually doing anything with them, children grow up so fast and time isn't guaranteed, so make beautiful memories together and cherish the time you have.

66 *NO BEAUTY SHINES BRIGHTER THAN THAT OF A GOOD HEART.* 99

Sometimes quiet people really do have so much to say but are careful who they open up to. Often there is not many people who are wise, my mum used to say – be careful who you trust, not everyone will have the same morals, intentions and values as us. Let go of anything that is bringing you down, try not to let negative circumstances deter you from good things your life has to offer.

You can change the situation by being the kind person that you are, never stop being the person you are, even when others do you wrong, just be yourself and let them be the person they want to be. I'm a great believer in the truth always comes out in the end. Sometimes things are not our fault but still our problem to deal with.

How you treat others says a lot about you and that's the real legacy you leave behind, how your kind heart touched so many souls. Be grateful for the people in your life who not only tell you they care, but show you they do.

Never waste a single day, time spent on yourself isn't wasted time. It is far better to be liked for who you really are then loved for who you aren't. Remember not everyone will appreciate your true opinions and not everyone is worth your opinion.

Choose to spend time with like-minded people, that truly bring you joy and are as pure as you. Happiness isn't about having the best of everything it's about making the most of what you have. You are not want others think you are in their heads. Don't put off the things you can do now.

When someone has a negative influence over any aspect of your life, you are giving them the power over you. Don't give anyone the power to destroy you! Inner peace and healing begins when you do not allow anyone or anything to control you.

Situations can change rapidly, life doesn't come with a manual, it comes with time that we learn from our experiences, to be happy we must learn to ignore people who think they know more about us than we do ourselves. When you find peace within yourself you find peace everywhere. Always count your blessings and practicing good gratitude is vital.

> **THE ONLY WAY TO DEAL WITH BULLIES IS TO STAND UP TO THEM**

Never allow anyone to hold the keys to your life. Be strong enough to realise what is right and what is wrong, be very careful and cautious of sharing your goals with anyone, avoid peer pressure and don't be afraid to say no, even when that may be standing alone. It is far better to be alone and happy than to be with the wrong company. Don't put yourself in situations where you don't feel comfortable with, trust your own vibes, your inner peace is much more important.

I personally know where I have attended functions for the sake of others even though my heart could not bear it, I put myself out for others who wouldn't even do that for me.

If lockdown taught me anything it was to embrace my life, believe in myself, enjoy my own space, the walks in nature and allow myself the time to slow down. Accept not everyone will value my existence and I shouldn't waste my energy trying to be recognised for the true person I am. It may have taught you different things, I never took or take anything for granted, as my mum taught me that from a young age.

You learn to listen to the energy from within, the universe is so powerful and you can manifest all that you desire, with your hard work, commitment, your mindfulness, well-being and happiness in mind.

Don't be afraid of what the future brings, your life isn't about the past, take control and only allow positivity to enter your soul. Anything that doesn't bring you peace needs to be addressed and left in the past, where it belongs.

I know that a lot of what happens to us isn't always in our control but how we choose to react ultimately is. It's okay to move on, close that chapter and walk away. If it is costing you your inner peace, it's not worth it. No one but you will know the exact details of what you have been through, many make up their own versions and many make up stuff when there's nothing to even say! Don't allow their versions define you and don't allow them to stand in your way, of what you're aiming to achieve in.

It's your life, you only have one life and go live it the best way, by being the best version of yourself. I always say people should live and let live.

Don't allow your kindness be mistaken as weakness. You are capable of whatever you desire, just be prepared to remove all the toxic people and things from your life and make space to embrace all the positive, good vibes and growth, all that you may have been putting on hold because of all the negativity your mind has had to deal with. Your mind can do anything if you set the mindset right.

"
REMEMBER THAT THE RELATIONSHIP YOU HAVE WITH YOURSELF AFFECTS ALL THE OTHERS.
"

It is extremely important that everyone in the household helps with all the chores and it is so disrespectful where in today's society many families still leave it to the women. If you have a family together the chores shouldn't be left to one person and while the rest continue to make a mess and not appreciate the hard work and multi duties that are on the shoulders of one person.

My mum used to say it's easier to go to work and have a break than it is to multi task several roles to run a household. She used to say, "for those who start it's never ending chores and things to do, there is always something else that needs doing and for those who don't start it's finished, as they can't see or be bothered to see what needs to be done."

She used to say it doesn't matter if you're a boy or a girl, we all get hungry, need clean clothes and have our needs, everyone needs to learn life skills and be able to look after themselves. She would say often people who don't want to really do a chore will do a rubbish job in hope they won't get asked to do it again, but they are the ones who need the experience and practice makes perfect! So let them keep doing things until they learn.

Many mothers put their lives on hold while the real lazy ones are too busy focusing on themselves or giving random strangers more attention than their own relationships, who don't even acknowledge their existence. Yet they fail to appreciate a good thing when it's right in front of them. We seem to live society where people are so obsessed with social media and the lives of others, usually fake yet very odd.

I hate when I'm out dining and I notice people on their phones on social media and not really engaging with the people they are supposed to be dining with, makes me so sad that people don't seem to value the importance of time and people right in front of them. I personally think life was better before social media and mobiles took over people's minds. It is very important to limit the use of gadgets I think. Even young children are seen with the mobile phones or gadgets given to them to keep them quiet and to occupy them. Why do people not seem to talk to each other in real life anymore?

I was taught to show gratitude all the time and particularly before eating a meal by my mum, today's society seem to think taking photos and posting everything online is the way to go. Bear in mind everyone you see online isn't real and you shouldn't compare your life to the life of others, you are unique.

Everyone has their limits and sometimes we must accept not everyone will appreciate our opinion or feelings, if we can't be truthful than we are not living a true life.

Truth is the key to being able to fully live the life we desire, if we can't be honest, we won't be able to live a fulfilled honest life. Life is not just about running around doing the millions of things for others, that we do without actually doing things for ourselves. We must be willing to experience aliveness together or it's going to hold you back, from living your best life.

> **66** *HONESTY IS THE BEST POLICY.* **99**

If the truth and willingness to live the life you dream is not there it is ok to let go, moving on isn't always a bad thing. It can be the beginning of the most amazing things in your life.

All relationships only work when the support, encouragement and freedom to pursue your dreams is equally there, when the respect, love, actions and appreciation is there, you deserve happiness, so don't allow anything less, every day is a second chance for you.

You are what you do not what you may say you do, actions speak louder than words. Criticising yourself won't help, instead approve of yourself and see what happens, if there is an area you're not happy with change it for yourself. You are capable of doing anything with the right mentality.

> **"** *YOU WENT THROUGH IT FOR A REASON...* **"**

We can't live according to our past, we must focus on the here and now, with positivity to live our best life. Life isn't always easy but how we deal with all aspects of it can be, if you practice regular meditation, recognise the signs of bad vibes, negativity, spiteful people and allow yourself to be in control of your own feelings, this will help you to deal with how you react to almost everything.

During our lifespan we will belong to a variety of different groups, relationships and clubs. This changes as we outgrow the interest, desire to be part of or move on to other areas in our life. Being part of something shouldn't make you feel like you are taking the wrong paths or be unhappy, recognise what is the good and what is just peer pressure.

My mum used to say relationships don't last unless two people work at it together and for the other to put the needs of their partner before their own, this is not to say that the one who has been sacrificing the most will keep doing so, if the other has never done the same or has ever shown any appreciation. Women get fed up she would say. All relationships in life require equal contribution for them to blossom, whether that is a friendship, work colleagues or any other.

My mum taught me so much throughout my life and she used to say, when one is moaning the other should stay quiet until they know it's a calmer time to have a civilised conversation! She used to say if two of you are working one of your salaries should be saved for security, as things can change in an instant.

If one is withholding their dreams, energy, hopes, truth, then they are likely to be very unhappy. You must be able to feel free in any relationship and if you are being held back from doing things for yourself and you have discussed this and nothing changes, chances are you are wasting your energy.

Everyone should know the right path for their life and don't allow others to mislead, misguide or bully you, you are unique.

You may feel you have weaknesses, limits and obstacles that will stop you from living the life you dream, but based on how we put our own mindset into action we can change our thoughts and change what our soul truly deserves. A positive mindset starts with you, learn to block, remove and move away from bad energy, bad vibes or feelings.

Smile, be happy and always count your blessings, not your problems. Look after yourself first. It's your life so make it a good one! Focus the mind on the good and good is all you should allow to come into your life. No one but you should decide what comes into your life, you deserve all the happiness, success and joy. I know that stress is part of our lives but we can still avoid overthinking things with negative views. We should acknowledge the issues and make a plan and decision on the best possible action to tackle it.

Learn to see the blessings that often come in disguise, in everything you experience and in all that you do. Prioritise your peace, respect yourself first and never allow anyone the opportunity to disrespect you over and over again.

Instead of living to get others to like you, live so you like yourself, be proud of yourself and be humble. Always share kindness, even when others don't show you that kindness. If you can't find a kind person, be that kind person. Spread kindness and always be kind to yourself. Do your best and accept it may not be enough for others, just praise yourself and be kind to yourself first.

Self-care and self-love is vital in a world where so many are suffering and so many are influenced by people's false identifies. The only person we need to impress is ourselves and with self-care in mind we can build ourselves up. It is not all easy and not always pleasant as we are the only person who has an impact on ourselves.

Sometimes the strength within is massive, it may be a little drop encouraging us to keep going, you got this.

> *I CHOOSE TO LOVE AND APPRECIATE MYSELF, MY INNER BEAUTY AND CHERISH MY MIND BODY AND SOUL FOR MYSELF ………*

Manifesting is something you allow.

Limits only exist in your mind, remember if you don't control your mind, someone else probably will.

Love yourself, honour and praise yourself for all you do daily. No one will ever love you like you need to love yourself. There is no need to be looking for someone to love you, you should be loving yourself fully first. Every new day is a day for new opportunities for you to rise and be positive for yourself. My mum used to say start the day with gratitude, thank God that you have woken up and you are able to open your eyes and see, hear and are able to get yourself up and ready.

The biggest impact is our mind first, don't allow the opinions of others defeat who you are, you are not what others say you are, you are unique and have your own purpose here in this world. Go live your dreams, make things happen and don't let anyone dull your sparkle.

You are not what people say you need to be, when we are able to recognise the comments, words, behaviour of others, we will become more aware of what we will allow and not allow. Often it can take many years to achieve the will power to realise who is genuine and who isn't. As my mum used to say a thief doesn't go around with a label saying that on their head!

Sometimes we can get so caught up in the situation that we don't see the difference between the people who actually really care and the ones who are just playing us.

In life people change, as with time, don't be afraid to allow new chapters to unfold and for you to move away from anything for anyone that doesn't bring you peace. Listen to your soul, it will never lie to you, believe in the gut instincts. Don't allow the words of others decide for you.

Self-care is the utmost important thing to every individual. Take time out and focus on taking deeps breaths, allow the negative vibes, thoughts, and anything that doesn't bring you peace to leave. Negative energy from others must be cleared from your mind in order for you to be happier for yourself.

Often being a strong minded person can make other people make so many assumptions about you, remember you are not what they think you are and you don't need to prove your worth to anyone, as long as you're a good person, earn an honest living, help those less fortunate then yourself and be kind, are the morals I was raised with and follow to this day.

I don't bother with petty people and their petty ways, once I'm done trying to help certain people see things from my view. If there's no hope, I focus on the real genuine people who are there for me and my family. I don't want to waste my energy where it's not appreciated or valued. Our time is very precious.

> **TRUST EVERYTHING THAT HAPPENS TO ME IS GOOD.**

Let go of hurt felt in the past, don't allow others to keep hurting you. Remember you choose what you are going to allow and not allow. This is your life and don't allow anyone to judge you, they aren't the ones who are walking in your shoes.

Your future is bright and good things are ahead, just allow the belief to be greater than the doubts. Truth is the best policy and I have the biggest respect for all those to follow the truth, even when telling the truth is painfully hard.

New days start with many new opportunities. Chase those dreams and go live the life you want, every day is a chance for a new opportunities. Meditation, breathing, journaling and finding what helps you relax is a lifelong gift, you can embrace it anytime, almost anywhere. For me even from a young age, I remember my mum giving me the most relaxing head massages. It is important we all make time to relax and to rejuvenate ourselves.

Most of the tradition relaxation has been around for centuries, like the Indian head massage, yoga and meditation to name a few.

66

INHALE & EXHALE.

99

All the little steps all add up to your end journey, as long as you keep moving towards your goal, you are getting where you need to be. Life doesn't have to be perfect to be wonderful. If it takes you longer than others, it doesn't mean it's impossible, or that you have failed, it won't happen, remember it's all about timing and you must always believe everything happens for a reason, even when we can't understand why at that moment in time. Everything that is written for us in our destiny will be for us and we must not let the problems that may occur on the way, put us off track to where we want to be.

Keep your soul rooted in gratitude. When we realise we aren't responsible for other people's behaviour, our intentions were pure, the love was true, but we may have been giving our all to the wrong people, who just keep breaking us. We must realise we are enough and we must take responsibility to stand up for ourselves and say that enough is enough, don't compare yourself to others, appreciate the unique special soul you are. If you're not happy with things and have discussed your feelings and nothing has changed, accept that others don't value or respect you enough to walk away.

Some people are just in a routine of misjudging us no matter how hard we try to explain things. My mum used to say so many people are full of jealously and it ruins things for themselves. When we are in situations where we don't feel loved, valued or appreciated our feelings change, remember the people who usually hurt you are not the people who will heal you.

It's going to be totally impossible to please them all, all the time, start by looking after yourself and your own mental well-being first. It's not a case of the glass being half empty for half full, be grateful you have a glass in the first place.

> **"**
> *LOGIC WILL TAKE YOU FROM A TO B, IMAGINATION WILL TAKE YOU EVERYWHERE.*
> *Albert Einstein*
> **"**

When we finally realise we are not the reason for someone else's wrong doings, that our intentions are pure, your love and commitment was real and utmost honest but it was all given to the wrong people, who just keep breaking you. Recognise the sights, do your best and realise when enough is exactly that, enough!

Don't try too hard being a people pleaser, you are likely to end up exhausted and it's like a dog chasing its own tail! Only please those that actually like to please you too and appreciate all that you do. It's a little bit like my mum used to say to me, don't drain yourself out doing things for others, when they clearly have no appreciation for my efforts or would never do the same for you.

Make the changes in your life for yourself and your inner peace, no one wants to live a life dealing with unnecessary stresses and strains, often we allow the behaviour of others ruin our peace, we must allow ourselves to create healthy boundaries and remove anyone or anything that is destroying our mental well-being, inner calm and peace of mind.

To improve your results in life, you must first improve your mental well-being, attitude and determination. Don't worry about the past or about any previous mistakes in life, just ensure you aren't making the same mistakes over and over again. First is a mistake, second is usually a choice.

Forgive yourself for accepting less than you deserve but be wise enough not to allow it to happen again. Learn to give yourself the love, care and attention you deserve, the care you have been giving to others, self-care is essential. Us mums, we tend to give our children all the attention and most fathers tend to be more selfish and do what suits them, however.

I do know of certain mothers who actually do their own thing and their children were not their main priority. Maybe it depends on who was your main role model during your own childhood. My mum was always there for me, that is why I felt it was not even questionable if I was going to be with her until I could. She was everything to me.

My mum used to say that you must be in your child(ren)'s present to be in their future. The bond needs to be formed for it to blossom. Many psychologist have researched on how the infants bond with their mother as she feeds them, so the connection starts way before a child can even speak. Many of you who are mothers may have noticed how a baby looks at the person who feeds them and they gain a great sense for that person, usually the main carer.

> **"**
> *SOMETIMES THE BRAVEST THING YOU CAN DO IS JUST BE YOURSELF EVERY ACCOMPLISHMENT STARTS WITH THE DECISION TO TRY.*
> **"**

Learn to let go of people and be happy to grow, move onto the next chapters of your life, for you. Be fearless, be kind and be you. Most people hate as they don't know how to value and love themselves. Most people would be better, if they focussed on their own real life than the one they seem to pretend to have online.

Don't always believe what you see, we seem to be living in a society where an image can be very misleading. It's what is in the inside that counts and we can be putting so much pressure on ourselves and from others to look a certain way to fit in. Someone will always have something to say about you either way. It's jealousy or admiration, don't let it concern you, you stay focussed on making things happen for you.

Keep Your Plans Private And Let Your Success Do The Talking!

The way you think and the conversations you will have with yourself have a huge impact on you actions, thoughts and can cause so much stress. Always be mindful of your thoughts. We can't control the actions of others but we can control the time and energy we give to negativity.

Remain balanced and focussed, listen to your own feelings, don't neglect self-care. Life will turn out better than you ever imagined if only you have the strength to follow your dreams and belief in yourself. Our biggest blessings often come in disguise, in everything you experience and even when it doesn't seem likely. Gratitude heals and be thankful for it all, all the time.

Don't let the hate and negativity of others bring you to their level, be grateful you aren't one of those people. People who have nothing good going on in their lives spend their time hating others, they just don't know how to love themselves so they usually look at blaming others for their horrid actions, behaviour and morals.

How they make you feel says a lot about them and nothing about you. If they can't say things directly to the individual it is about, then they shouldn't be saying it at all.

Accept you're not going to be for everyone, accept you are unique and you have standards. Accept it and like it. Create the boundaries and don't allow others to break them at a cost of you own peace. Often the helpers are so focussed on helping others that they forget about helping themselves. Always make time for the things that make you happy.

Be the best version of yourself for yourself, no one matters as much as you do for yourself. Self-care should be a priority and not just something we do time to time, after let downs or disappointments.

When people show you they don't care believe them, don't try to help or make them see sense, it's often said, "You don't know what you had until it's gone," and the fact is most of these people get stuck in their own selfish ways that they don't even know it.

One thing I learnt the hard way, is that no matter how much I do for some people they won't actually do the same back for me, I may have made them a priority but they won't see me as a priority, the world seems to be full of people who remember you when they need you but don't make the time for us if we need them. The world seems to be all about using people as things and the love of things is becoming greater than the love of people.

My mum used to say it's easy for so many to walk away from their responsibilities but it takes more of a heart to forgive and try to help. Listen to all but do what feels right for your heart she would say.

There are many little things my mum used to do and I still do them myself, if she was to gift money in a card for an occasion, she would make it to always add the one pound like, £11, £21, £51 or £101 as to represent never forget the one. Another tradition was never return an empty Tupperware to anyone, gift an empty purse or wallet. Many may say this is just superstitions but I go with what feels right.

Just be yourself and don't let anyone dull your sparkle.

So it's best to always think of your own happiness and well-being before you put yourself out for anyone, unless of course they are the rare few who are always there for you, no matter what. If you have these people in your life cherish them as they are far a few, they are rare and unique. As long as they are honest, loyal, respectful and caring they are special.

Never drain yourself out pleasing the ungrateful.

My mum used to say if they are going to talk about you they will, regardless if it's good or bad, they just got to talk. Most of the time they don't even know the truth but still like to discuss others. You need to know what should be addressed and what should be ignored. You inner peace is worth more than other people's bad habit of spreading gossip.

In today's societies we seem to live in a very selfish world, whereas I remember the lovely memories of a busy household in my mum's house, the doors were always open to guests coming and going. On the weekends, my mum was prepared for any unexpected guests and always knew the atmosphere was always so happy and welcoming. She would say in years to come no one will go to anyone without an invitation.

I tend to avoid people or places where I feel unwelcome, if there's a bad vibe it isn't worth my time! If you find yourself in situations where you are going for the sake of it, don't, as nothing is worth more than your own well-being, we put so much pressure on our own mental well-being to please others that they wouldn't even care less about us.

Don't put yourself in situations where you feel so uncomfortable and unhappy, your inner peace is worth more than anything.

When the behaviour, events and actions of others let us down it is easy to get into a self-blame routine, easy to think we can't ever be happy, trust or love again, but the truth is we shouldn't be giving so much of ourselves to those who don't value our existence. Often we are so harsh on ourselves that we forget that self-care is essential for our mental well-being.

Get into a good morning routine of waking up early to meditate, pray and stretch. Having a set bedtime is also just as important. Always count your blessings and start you day with positivity, gratitude and allow your heart to be filled with kindness.

Write things down to practice gratitude, healing is a daily process. Everything is connected to this universe and your soul can sense a lot more than you may realise. Look at how much you are capable of. All aspects of your life can blossom with good vibes, you are going to be the only one who will be your biggest supporter in this journey of life.

You are about to be happier, if only you allow yourself to follow your heart and listen to your inner voice. There is no need to stress or worry about all the things we cannot control.

Being self-detractive is the best way to give yourself the best compassion, love and attention you deserve. Allow yourself to put yourself first and listen to your own needs.

> **KNOW WHICH BRIDGES ARE WORTH FIXING AND WHICH ARE NOT.**

Inner peace, acceptance and realise your mental well-being is vital, if something is draining you, holding you back or causing you too much pain let it go, feel your soul and be happy to embrace the new chapters in your life. No one deserves to feel so suffocated, trapped or unhappy because of the actions, behaviours and lack of respect of others.

Focus on the things you like and the things that make you happy, a positive mindset is what attracts us to a positive life.

We shouldn't focus on criticising others, we should remain focussed on positive thoughts, starting with ourselves. Yes I know you're thinking, how this is possible if others are doing wrong, focus on thinking and talking only happy and positive thoughts, except we can't control the feelings of others towards us but we can focus on our thoughts and actions.

Your worth is not based on the opinion of others.

I know it's been tough but I hope you aren't being tough on yourself, be kind to yourself and to this around you. Positive self-talk and positive procrastination is a must.

Change the way you think and change your whole mindset. Kindness shared will bring kindness back. Learn to let go of anything that doesn't feel right for you. Focus on your self-worth.

Daily positive journaling is good and stay positive all the time. Life is like a story full of chapters, just don't be afraid to turn the pages or you may miss something. Don't hold onto something that's holding your own happiness at the expense of your own peace.

Accept not everyone will deserve a piece of your good heart, your good intentions, kindness and care, sometimes we can find ourselves holding onto things when it is not valued, appreciated or returned. Not everyone has a good heart and soul, sometimes if we give too much to ungrateful people they simply get comfortable with their own selfish ways.

Allow yourself to be happy, free and live a peaceful life, you can only take responsibility for your own actions, not the actions of those around you. Since covid-19 many people have had the things they may have taken for granted taken away from them and circumstances changed instantly for many people around the globe.

My mum used to tell me to always remember to be grateful to the good lord above and that to never take anything for granted, as when the universe wants to change things, it will do, without any warning and within a second. That stuck with me for life and Covid-19 is a perfect example how true that is.

I was taught to always be thankful for a roof over my head, food to eat, clean clothes to wear, etc., many things people in today's societies may take for granted. In today's societies people seem to be more obsessed with taking photos of our food to post online, live their life spending hours scrolling online looking at other people, often strangers' lives online than actually valuing their own or those close to them.

It is such a sad way of living often adding negative pressure on ourselves and forgetting the people who are actually in your presence, giving strangers more attention than those who should be your nearest and dearest.

Not to mention the bad habits and routine many phone addictions get into, they seem to worship their mobiles more than their own health, the time spent scrolling online is not recognised by many as the contents are not page numbers and do not require to physically turn the pages and our brains don't realise the amount of time that can be spent scrolling, what we look at goes into minds and affects our lifestyle. Even though a lot of online content can be fake.

Far too many people are in very bad habits now that they don't actually have real conversations anymore, how often do you see people out together and the phone is getting the most attention! Time is precious and the people we are blessed with are precious too, none of us actually know when will be the last time we get to actually see those people, so don't get into ridiculous bad habits of giving your phone more attention than real people, the real people who are supposed to be your loved ones, show them that love and not the love for your phone.

I hate to think the amount of people who spent far too much time with their mobiles all day than, carry it like it's their lifeline, it's the last thing they scroll through at night and the first in the morning! Nothing worse than making real people feel invisible while they spend hours giving randoms more attention.

Then people complain they have no energy, no time and no knowledge of what's actually going on in front of them. The fact is if people get into all the bad habits it becomes a habit that they can't break as they keep feeding their mind and body the wrong energy. It is said it takes 21 days to break a habit, in today's society most people can't leave their phones for 21 seconds without a twitch!

Changing our routines and changing our habits is a good starting point, reading is far more better for the mind then scrolling online, you will become far more happier if you wake up and spent a few minutes mediating, take a walk in nature, avoid gadgets and do things that will lighten the mind to allow you to focus on the day ahead.

Showing gratitude that you have been blessed with another new day. A new day to make some change to the world, and Gandhi says, "'Be the change that you wish to see in the world." It starts with you.

It is surprising the amount of people who can't actually connect with their own company solo, no one will have as much conversations, as the conversations you are going to have with yourself and your inner voice.

Make the contents from the outside world positive so the inside conversations are positive as well. Focus on your health as that's the biggest wealth you have.

> **"**
> *HELP ME EMBRACE WHATEVER*
> *LIFE BRINGS ....*
> *HAPPINESS AND SELF LOVE*
> *IS MEDICINE.*
> **"**

We all would be happier if we could be focussed on the positive aspects of life, my mum used to be so strong minded and would tell me to always look at the positives in life, even during the most painful times, she taught me to turn the negatives into a positive and that often we don't understand, where things are going in a certain way but to have faith and believe whatever God is doing for us, it's all for the good.

The universe is very powerful. We need to be strong enough to believe in our abilities, remove toxic people, remove ourselves and our thoughts away from other people's behaviour, focus on our own well-being and ensure we listen to what our heart is telling our minds. Overthinking can ruin everything and will resolve nothing. Believe in your gut instincts. Often we can create a problem for ourselves simply by giving our energy to something that doesn't exist and our thoughts will spend the energy on it when it could be spent elsewhere, on much more positive aspects of life.

Be mindful of your thoughts and be cautious of what can follow them. It's never too late to live the life you dream of, your dreams are important and you deserve peace and happiness. You don't need to say yes to everything and don't dwell on the past.

Think of your life as a blank canvas and only add what you want on there, use your vision to create the life you want and do not add anything that doesn't feel right. Remember how far you have come, don't give up, keep your dreams alive. Whatever you are achieving in life is heading the right way as long as you keep believing in yourself, just keep moving.

Take breaks when you feel exhausted, don't wait for others to notice your needs, they may never notice, learn to make yourself a priority. Self-care is vital, I know it can also be difficult with so much going on, but mum guilt seems to be real. As mums, at least most mums, we put everyone and everything before our own needs, often we forget to recognise we are important as well and our well-being is very important. If we don't look after ourselves how are we going to look after anything else.

We must not feel guilty and our mental health is so important. Have you ever felt like you want to take away someone's pain? To make them feel okay, to give them so much love and make sure they never feel sad or hurt again. If so do try doing that for yourself first.

Sometimes we get so caught up in our routines, comfort zones that we forget to allow ourselves to grow. Dare to dream and dare to believe.

> **IF YOU DON'T EXPECT IT DONE TO YOU DON'T DO IT TO OTHERS.**

Practice gratitude as much as possible, with all your heart for all that you have had, have and want in the future. Be grateful for everything and everyone in your life, never take anything or anyone for granted. We can lose far too much due to unappreciation.

The more we thank people for their help the more people want to help, simple things as starting with thanking all.

I am so thankful for the mother I was blessed with, the time I had with her and the amount of love, attention, memories and things she taught me. I am thankful for my family and friends, thankful for a roof over my head and for everything I am blessed with, from clean water to drink to being able to see and write this today.

Gratitude is the core of our own happiness and peace, my mum taught me this from a young age. She also taught me to always be happy for other people's happiness and success and you will allow good things to come into your own life.

A simple routine as you wake up in the morning is to think of how fortunate and privileged you are to have a life, to be alive. Start your days with gratitude, count your blessing not your problems. Be kind to all around you, help those around you and be appreciative to all.

Little acts of kindness go a long way, never look down on others and value each and every person you meet, regardless of their job title, appearance or status. It is so good to see people earning an honest living and as a Sikh myself, I honour the three core tenets of my religion, meditation upon and devotion to the creator, truthful living, and service to humanity.

Being real is far more important than trying to be perfect, Be happy every second is precious. Don't feel guilty for removing people who don't feel good for your soul, wish them well and move on. You can't change people's opinions of you and you shouldn't allow it to concern you. I trust vibes, not words. You are able to achieve anything you put your mind to, you just got to give yourself the credit you deserve and you are the only one who will be your greatest believer. Remove all the doubts, the negativity and anything that does not feel good for the soul, the vibes needs to be good.

Always remind yourself that you will be okay and everything will work out for you as you have wanted. What is meant for you will be, however you must remove negativity and replace it all with love and gratitude to blossom. The more we love the more the love returns to us, just like good deeds are a good practice.

Don't be afraid to ask for help, get the support or talk to a good reliable person. Sometimes we can think we are alone and others will judge us, but we shouldn't shy away from our true feelings and needs. Seeking help doesn't make us weaker, it shows we are able to connect with ourselves and we are putting our mental health at the forefront. It is part of how we will feel better, move forward and accept things.

"
I'M RESPONSIBLE ABOUT THE WAY I FEEL ABOUT MYSELF.
"

Don't be afraid to grow, remember what you deserve and what you want to achieve in this precious life of yours.

It is often said when people hurt you, it is a sign that something is wrong with them, they may not accept their faults but look at blaming others. Except we cannot change someone who can't see anything wrong with their behaviour, allow yourself to move away.

When others lie to us over and over again, we usually start to doubt everything they say, Compulsive liars are the worst and liars with a bad memory are just at another level! Don't let them use the guilt trip on you and twist the truth as the true always comes out in the end, and whatever we shall harvest we shall consume.

My mum used to tell me to walk away from anyone who mistreats me over and over again, don't allow them too many chances as they become comfortable with thinking another chance will follow. Once is a mistake, after that it's usually a choice. She would say life is such a precious gift and it shouldn't feel like a sentence.

It is far better to be alone than it is to be with the wrong company. Closure is a blessing if it is causing you too much pain. Live life as if you were to die tomorrow, die at peace with your soul, not regrets. You just need to trust yourself and stay focused on the important things in your life.

When they don't value your presence give them the gift of your absence.

Good people are hard to come by, fake people are everywhere! We need to recognise our circle and keep it real, keep in small and keep it kind. I rather remove myself from people or situations that I don't feel valued, comfortable or welcome with, as there's nothing worse than feeling out of place. Good vibes only please.

No one can stop your blessings from manifesting. Positive vibes, positive soul, happy thoughts, gratitude and remember you are doing amazing. Peaceful mind and peaceful life.

People who happy for others simply because they are doing well and are happy, are my kind of people. The power of happiness is within us all, it's not about assets, it's about our own mindset, the more we appreciate the little things, we realise they are actually the big things. Some may be taking things for granted, but the more we will learn the importance of gratitude the better we feel.

Remember what you may take for granted someone around the universe is probably praying hard for.

66
LIFE IS GOOD BECAUSE OF THE CHOICES AND SACRIFICES WE MADE
99

Don't let the bad vibes, negativity of others ruin or delay your plans, if it's your dream, go chase them with all your heart, when your soul is happy, your energy will give you the strength to keep focussed.

Often the people we feel we can share things with, are the ones who secretly envy us, hold us back and want to control our destiny, it is not there's to live, it's yours. Quite often the signs may not get noticed immediately but in time you may notice, how the support is not there for you and how much other distractions are placed your way, you will realise.

Those who truly love you respect you enough to be honest all the time, even when honestly is hard. When you love yourself unconditionally you set the standards and the boundaries for the rest of the world, and you will have the strength to not allow anyone or anything to come in your way.

Keep your plans close to your heart and don't share things too soon with anyone, but yourself. Remember you are your biggest supporter and you are what you do and not what you say you will do. Take action to get to where you feel is your happy place, don't tell others your plans show them with your actions, your success, your progress, all at your own pace for yourself and for those who are so near and dear to your heart and soul.

Live life at your own pace, don't stress, we are all unique and everything will happen when the time is right for us. Be patient, have faith, be loyal, be trusting, be loving, be honest and be yourself.

All we have is now, learn from yesterday, live for now and hope for tomorrow, nothing is eternal, be true to yourself and others. Celebrate every little victory and be proud of it too.

If you put your mind to something, you will achieve it, but only if you believe in it, then the rest will follow. Let yourself grow and blossom daily, avoid guilt, disbelieve, negativity and allow your mind to think is a good way always.

We can't control everything around us, but we can control our own actions. What is going to happen will happen, use your energy on what is within your control, worrying about what could or would happen won't change it. Stay humble, wisdom comes quietly.

> **LET THEM MAKE THEIR OWN MISTAKES, LET THEM LEARN OR NOT LEARN.**

Your life, mind & soul can change instantly, we must be ready to take time to care for our own well-being, therefore we can help our family, friends and others. We are not going to be of any use to anyone, if we can't help ourselves first. Only then will you be able to move onto the next chapter in your life.

Take accountability of what was going on in your life, I don't mean you blame yourself, but recognise what's going on, or how you want to move on from the past, accept things by understanding learn from mistakes, but do not allow yourself to get in a rut of repeating past mistakes. Leave the past behind in history where it belongs. Don't keep awakening the past mistakes, let them rest but do not repeat them. Learn from them and move in a different direction.

Take things at your pace. We all should have the right to be able to speak about our mental health, without any judgement, punishment or guilt.

Our brains are extremely busy, collecting information and it is not surprising it can feel so exhausting. Don't be afraid to ask for help. Pause from life and listen to your own body, aches and pains, lack of sleep, inability to have the energy to do things, can all be signs of your body trying to tell you something, you might be simply ignoring the signs.

You can literally feel when it is time to stop, breathe and relax to revive and save yourself, your inner peace.

Don't compare yourself to others, we all will get to where we want to be, when the time is right. Take the right steps and make the right plans, however big or small, praise yourself for working towards the end result. Reward yourself for all that you are achieving, gaining, improving and growing through.

Make time for yourself feel your own vibe, enjoy life, a peaceful life is better than being with the wrong people. Remember not everyone will appreciate you, but that's okay. Life is too short to tolerate people or things that cause you strain and make you unhappy. Put an end to the excess baggage, your shoulders don't need the heavy load.

Surround yourself with people who actually genuinely care, don't feel you need people around you to be happy, embrace happiness starting with you. It is better to be alone than it is to be with the wrong people.

Don't give people too many chances that they feel comfortable with their mistakes and think you will give them another chance, no matter what wrong doings they do.

> **" BE PROUD OF THE PERSON WHO LOOKS BACK AT YOU IN THE MIRROR. "**

Never talk negatively about yourself, words are energy and you must think about how you speak to yourself. Change the way you speak to yourself and you can change your life. What you don't change is a choice you are making to keep.

Having a good clear vision is good and only keep things that actually bring you joy, have sentimental value or are special to you. Be the best version of yourself for yourself.

Less clutter in your home, less clutter in your mind, less clutter in your way and less clutter overflowing your head! Less really is more. Don't feel you need to follow anyone, remember who you are, live and let live. Self-love is vital, accept yourself fully.

I never understand why some people are so competitive in all the wrong ways, like why do they feel that they must have the same things, do the something or go to places as others do?

Find your own people who inspire you to be a better version of yourself. Clear things out that are not creating happy memories or gifts from people who aren't creating good vibes!

Like your home, clear things from your mind and your social media, diaries and anywhere you are holding onto the negative vibes. Nothing worse than getting gifts from people who aren't really happy to give you these with good intentions, or from people who ask for them back!! Seriously don't bother to give them in the first place, it's not like materialistic things can bring you any joy.

Keep the vibes right and create the right vibes as much as you can.

When our minds are overflowing with information it is hard to relax, focus on a particular task. I often find myself wondering in my thoughts, especially when I try to sleep, I have found myself blaming myself for the behaviour of others, my to-do lists keep growing and my mind overflows with information. I find listening to calm relaxing sleep music helps my mind to stop over thinking. I strongly recommend you try what helps you feel relaxed, ignore all negative impact of others, consider it as lots of noise, annoying noise, interfering your inner peace.

It's your life, your mind, body and soul, no one will be there for you like you should be there for yourself. Meditation is good for your soul, energy doesn't lie.

66
GOOD VIBES ONLY PLEASE
99

Believe in the gut instincts, feel the right vibe. Spend time with those who bring the best in you, not the stress in you.

> 66
> *ALWAYS SMILE AND YOUR MIND WILL SMILE WITH YOU, BELIEVE IN YOURSELF.*
> 99

I'm a strong believer that having a clean and organised home, helps create a better structure and encourage everyone to use a little bit of initiative to maintain good life skills & morals.

Listening to uplifting relaxing music is good for your mind. Find what makes you feel at ease and pursue that more and more...... Our minds start to believe what we tell it over and over, it will start to believe whatever information we transfer into our minds and thoughts.

Be careful with your words. Be clear of what you want and don't want. Always count your blessings. Change your mindset, raise your standards and allow negativity to leave your thoughts, do not doubt what you can achieve, what you can do and how you plan to get there. Most great things start with a single idea!

Remember it takes 21 days to break habits. Our brains are strong, how we choose to transfer the data into it will have a big impact on your life. Try to only have positive information going into your mind and thoughts. Yes I know it is hard to remain positive all the time, often not in our control but how we react to the information and how to decide to store it will have a huge impact, on your well-being. We must ensure we take time to only give our energy to what we want to manifest further.

Allow things to enter and leave the mind if it's not helping you. Our brains are not programmed permanently to stay stuck, we can reprogram it.

Change your focus, change your mindset, focus on your positives, believe in the ability to live stress free, rearrange your own thinking and allow what you can't control to not destroy your inner peace. Don't be afraid in transforming your life for the better.

You can achieve abundance if you put your intelligence to good use. I don't mean the intelligence you have achieved through educational certificates, I am referring to all the thoughts in your mind, with subconsciously and the conscious mind.

Our intentions will create what we actually want, don't limit your beliefs, believe you can do, get and achieve what you want to manifest in your life. Stop wasting time on what others think of you, your self-expressions, freedom to self, self-awareness and to truly be yourself needs you to be able to be yourself. No matter what the situation is, unapologetically at all times, without worrying whilst others think, regardless of how others choose to perceive you.

Remember the mind is a very sharp tool and your body is strong. Love yourself, except yourself for everything that you are. Remember you can't control the behaviour of others, only how you react to them. Best to ignore things we cannot control. Don't let it destroy your inner peace.

> **"**
> *ONE SKILL TO MASTER IS HOW YOU TALK TO YOURSELF KINDLY.*
> **"**

Stay where your soul feels happy.

When you start to get better at talking to yourself kindly, you may feel sad to begin with at how hard we were on ourselves, how the action of others failed us, we often blame ourselves for the things that are out of our control. We must not beat ourselves up, but learn to be kinder to ourselves. Often healing involves healthy grieving. Take time to heal, be kind, honest and thoughtful to yourself.

The messages we send to ourselves the pain we feel in our body is all to do with how we talk to ourselves.

Always practice gratitude, start your day with positive thoughts, actions and plans, happy thoughts will uplift your mood, start with deep breathing meditation, gratitude and prays. Your day will feel uplifted and your heart will feel full of kindness.

Happiness, success, belief all starts from within, that's up to you on how you can control your inner voice, inner peace and your inner soul. Leave the history behind and start from now with a better version of yourself for yourself. It's about your life story but we all need to be able to communicate with ourselves in a positive way. Don't be afraid to set high standards for yourself.

Start with a different reality of how you communicate with yourself the right way, guide yourself with positive vibes to power your thoughts, so you are much more in control with your emotions, then you can make better life choices.

It's a lifetime journey to master the importance of persistence to how you talk to yourself, that inner voice thoughts and nagging sounds. Be aware of your daily thoughts and the action, energy you give it will have a huge impact on you daily.

So much of what happens to us and what we do is an impact of how we talk to ourselves. The most important conversations you'll ever have are those that you have with yourself.

My mum used to say as women, we have so many roles not just one job which everyone can do, one job she would say. We are always going to put the needs of our children first, (not all mothers, I know). We are the doctors, nurses, teachers, caretakers, chef, taxi, housekeeper, artist, play leader, counsellor, etc.

We all have so many pressure on ourselves, we feel guilty for taking time out for ourselves, we should be more like men! Sorry if you are a good all rounder and a man.

None of us are perfect and we all have different morals.

> **66**
> *WE MUST MAKE TIME TO BE IN OUR CHILDREN'S PRESENCE TO BE IN THEIR FUTURE.*
> **99**

Present time is a gift, hence why it's called the present. Today give yourself some love, care, patience and compassion. Praise yourself for all that you do, all that you are and all that you are becoming. Sometimes things may go wrong for us is actually, leading us to better beginnings. Let it go.

Life changes, we think we are losing people. Friends, things, ourselves but we are actually becoming better, better friends, better people and a better, wiser and stronger you is shaping up. Do not be afraid to lose toxic friends, people, groups, etc. If it is costing you your inner peace than it isn't worth it.

The life you are dreaming about can all happen, you just have to make the right choices to make it work. You can't wait for everything to change and then you'll believe it, you must have the right mindset and believe it to achieve it. Your destiny is not based on your history.

Loving yourself first is the key to everything, give yourself the same time and attention as you give to everyone else. You are worthy of all the good things, cherish who you are and your life is a gift and so is your time. Be your own cheerleader, best friend, coffee buddy, own soul mate, your own everything, rather than relying on others. You will become happier in your own presence.

I love solo walking, meals, walks in nature, having alone time and the sound of silence. It is amazing how much you will actually connect with your own soul and hear your own thoughts clearer.

Make that time of living with an open mind, a happy heart and being kind to yourself. It is necessary. Learn to have the patience and trust the timing of the universe while you connect yourself in self-care, self-worth and self-love. Just remember the life you are dreaming of is possible, even in our difficult times in life, trust what is yet to come.

Not only should we be more wise, careful and particular about the people we allow into our lives, but we should look at all aspects that bring energy into it from other avenues.

What we read, watch, listen to or spend hours doing, all have psychological impact on our minds and behaviours. It is better to be alone than to be with the wrong people, places, habits, etc.

According to psychology when we focus on problems, we create more problems, when we change our mindset and look at the possibilities, we will have more opportunities. A bit like when we say life is what you made it.

> **66** *UNTIL IT IS YOUR TURN KEEP CLAPPING FOR OTHERS SIMPLE* **99**

My mum use to always say that people can cover the eyes of others, but God watches us all, all of the time and we cannot cover that fact. Having faith is very good for the soul and it gives me a sense of belonging. If you follow the good intentions, it is a good way of meditation and the reassurance of never being alone.

Remember your peace is far more important, when you find yourself reacting to something or someone, that doesn't deserve your energy or time. We are not responsible for other people's behaviours.

A wise person once said be careful who you allow on to your ship, because some people will sink the whole ship because they can't be captain.

Set yourself healthy boundaries and be firm. Nothing wrong with knowing when you have had enough, sometimes nothing we say or do is being received with good intentions. Not everyone can see a good heart and some people just don't like you but I know it is hard when they don't even know the real you.

Be cautious of giving people too many chances, as often these people become disrespectful of your genuine caring heart and use it against you. Fake people seem to go round trying to ruin the good souls, just so they can believe the lies that live within them, to make themselves look good.

I'm a great believer in that the truth always comes out in the end, let these people think their stories, lies and comments of you is the truth.

Don't get caught up in a materialistic life, help others who are less fortunate than yourself. Don't get me wrong if you want certain things get them with your own hard work, don't sit thinking you can brag what you have when deep down you know you haven't worked for it. No one should envy others and no one should look down on others.

66
THE ONLY THING WE HAVE IS MOMENTS IN TIME......
99

My mum use to always tell me to be forever grateful for everything, from having a roof over my head, food, clothes, health to the shoes on my feet, etc. I'm the same with my children. My mum used to say everything can change with a click of a finger and I'm sure with the covid-19 pandemic many would agree, although we still have plenty of ungrateful people around, who never seem to learn the importance of gratitude, blessings and kindness.

WE COME EMPTY HANDED, WE GO EMPTY HANDED......

There is no greater feeling than achieving things and forwarding yourself and others from your hard work. Everyone seems to be there for you when you are known to others, have money and success but your true real people are the ones who didn't leave you when they no longer needed you or you didn't benefit from their use of you.

Work hard for your own assets don't look at others and hope it will be yours. No one has the right to think they are entitled to anything, I would rather give my assets to a charity than to a ungrateful person, if they were not there for you while you were alive than they don't deserve your assets either.

> " *YOUR LEGACY IS ALL THAT GETS LEFT HERE.* "

My mum used to say how many people don't bother with a person while they are alive but turn up with flowers when they have passed away, she would say "it's not like they are going to collect these from you now". Losing my mum is so painful and I'm deeply heartbroken to this day. It is like my mum used to say, only the good lord knows when is the day we go and it is all written before we are even born.

She would say how people are becoming very materialistic these days and that people seem to forget we come empty handed and we go empty handed. The only thing we leave behind is what our nearest and dearest say about us, I'm not talking about the ones who were never there for us during our lives. The ones who actually know the real you, cared about you and you left an impact on their lives.

> **WHERE THE FOCUS GOES THE ENERGY FLOWS.**

My mum would say things to me about certain people and how they will be nearby when she has passed, just for assets. When I go to rest at the end of each day, I often get thoughts and dreams of my mum, which I feel is a sign she is always watching over me.

Bereavement is a very difficult experience and it all depends on your relationship with the person. Don't go over things that cannot be changed, all the what if, what about to name a few. As long as you did everything in your power for that person while they were here that is all you could have done.

Believe everything happens for a reason and although death is hard and very painful, I know what limited strength I had to keep my mum, right until 4am when the nurse in critical care came over and told me there is nothing more they can do to help my mum. I felt so useless, so alone and powerless, shattered and shocked.

Trust takes years to build and can be turned in seconds. When I think of my mum, I think of all the amazing things she taught me. The love she gave, she was the kindest person, she was open, honest, loyal, caring, grateful, religious and truly a beautiful mother. I was truly blessed to be her daughter.

When you have such a special bond, that bond cannot be broken, even after death do us part. I am so attached to my mum to this day, although I can't see, speak or touch her, I miss the physical contact, hearing her voice, her singing while cooking. I try to keep her memories alive with all that she taught me, with daily conversations about her, her photos and all the little things I have that she brought me in my kitchen, cardigans she has knitted for me to her special items of clothing.

I no longer am a people pleaser, as my mum use to say, "It's impossible to please them all, all the time," so I now do what is right for my own peace of mind.

My priorities are my children, I give them the same advice that my mum taught me and more, as society has too many other negative influences nowadays. My mum used to say to me, "it is not you I don't trust but it is society". We can only give the advice, it will be respected or neglected. I was a firm believer in respect the freedom you get and gain more, abuse it and you lose it. I miss my mum every second, I am thankful I had such an amazing mum. She is such an inspiration to me and always will be.

My mum used to say people stop making time for you when the need of you changes. Some people don't like the version of you that is in their head, that's okay as they don't even know you. My mum would always turn every negative into a positive situation.

" PROTECT WHAT YOU LOVE FROM THE EVIL EYE OF OTHERS. "

The actions of others who hurt her to the end, but she told me in hospital that by hurting her she realises how little they respected all that she had done and that taught me to follow what she used to say, 'Love and respect is a two way thing, some don't know how to give it and some don't know how to receive it.'

I 100% agree with this saying and often when some people hurt me, I blamed myself for their actions, but now I am happy to cut people off, for my own peace of mind and inner calm, not everyone is I suppose.

Learn to accept that and move on, yes, easier said than done, I hear you say! Do what feels good for your soul. Nothing is worth more than your health and mental well-being.

> **"**
> *YOU CAN'T KEEP SAYING SORRY,*
> *IF YOU KEEP DOING WHAT*
> *YOU'RE SUPPOSE TO*
> *BE SORRY FOR.*
> **"**

I genuinely feel happy for others when they are happy. Maybe it is just me, but I know my mum was the same. She use to say be happy for others and God gives you more too. She was always happy for others and to put a smile on the faces of others.

My mum had the purest heart ever known to me. She would have tea ready for our postman when it was cold outside, she would have lunch ready for her medical supply delivery drivers. The acts of kindness were amazing and she never once expected anything in return.

Truly blessed are those who knew her, those who live by her teachings and those who are learning from her knowledge.

My mum passed away on the 2nd of December 2002, a day my whole life shattered in front of my eyes. Long live her legacy that she has left behind.

When I talk about the things my mum taught me, her quotes to others and tell people, so many people have told me how lucky I was, to have such an amazing mother. I couldn't agree more.

I have learnt how being positive is such a good feeling and that you will flutter like a butterfly yourself. Life is full of stressful situations, but how we learn to acknowledge it and deal with it is all about our mindset. It is part of our daily life and what one person may find stressful the other may think it is a breeze. Go with the flow isn't always the option, dealing with it will an open heart and putting your needs out there is. If it is costing you your peace of mind it is not worth it.

Never get too comfortable mistreating anyone or anything, everyone has their limits and you may not realise until it's too late. Be kind and if you can't be kind don't be cruel. Seek help for areas in your life that are causing you to continuously hurt others or even yourself.

Appreciate what you have and the universe will give you more. When you are happy it is such a magical feeling and you will glow differently yourself. My mum used to say, 'Remember not everyone is raised the same way,' we often expect what we think is the norm from others, but can be disappointed when it isn't. However we all should know what kindness is, what is right & wrong. We all should feel responsible if we are causing unnecessary pain, stress, worry or hurt others, too many people cause their own dramas in life, but so many innocent people get caught up in it or suffer from the actions, behaviour and comments of others.

We can't be responsible for the behaviour of others. We must either learn from our mistakes or we tend to keep repeating them. More people need to be honest to themselves than they may be able to be honest with others.

I believe it is better to be hated for what you really are then to be loved by pretending to be something you aren't. I also believe the truth always comes out in the end. If you get into bad habits of lying no one will believe you when you actually tell the truth either. Chances are the person or people you are lying to will already know the truth and by lying to them it will jeopardise the relationship, often beyond repair.

Relationships only work when both parties are equally committed to each other, as for all relationships. Most people don't know what they have until it is gone or they didn't appreciate what they had and thought they would have it forever. Nothing lasts forever, it is just our way of expressing to the end of our lifetime.

What most people fail to notice is that there is so much negative influences in their lives, often they can't see the bad grapes from the good, never believe everything you see online and never compare your life with other peoples.

Most insecurities can be from a person's childhood and upbringing. So many scars left unhealed that they cannot accept or recognise a good thing when it is right in front of their face. Therapy should be considered if you feel you need it.

We only have one life and the behaviour of others can have such a negative impact on us and our own well-being. My mum use to say to me that it is not me she don't trust, but it's the society. That has stuck with me to this day, I have said this to my own children as well as others. She would also say a thief doesn't go around with it written on their forehead!

To me I have always tried to protect my relationship with others, the world seems to be filled with negative people, jealous, bitter people, fake and interfering bodies! But that isn't the solution if the others are not in the same boat. It is like the saying, "You scratch my back and I will scratch yours."

In any relationship both people must be willing to put the happiness of the other before themselves, but if it is not getting the appreciation or meant halfway there comes a point where the giver will get exhausted and feel they are wasting their time. Time is a very precious gift, one that can't be returned. You can't control everything, sometimes you just need to relax and have faith that things will work out, let what will be, be and what won't be, go.

In today's society more and more people are unfaithful, they are too busy looking elsewhere than investing in what's in front of them, focussing on what isn't important. Relationships only work when both partners have similar or the same priories. I feel if they have similar priorities more so than hobbies, individuals will also look at what is their main priority in their lives, not just the life of one person.

The problem with modern day dating there is no space for error, people move on too quickly without giving it time. My mum use to say, 'You only have to sneeze and people file for a divorce.' But the flip side to that is giving too many chances to the wrong people will drain you out mentally and being with them will make you extremely unhappy, and affect your mental well-being. Remember relationships only work when both people work at it together and support each other no matter what.

> **" BREATHE, LET GO, REMIND YOURSELF THIS VERY SECOND IS ALL THAT WE TRULY HAVE. "**

If some people put as much energy as they do into their phones, social media and other people's lives, they may actually be a little more productive in their own.

Women in particular can put their life on hold to spend years running around others, often these other people don't even notice how much a mother does, they become ignorant, lazy and ungrateful. To all the lazy people, get up, wake up and at least pick up after your own mess. Never underestimate how much a mother does, especially if you know she runs around you and others with all her heart.

Those of you in relationships or have children, don't be selfish and remember you chose to bring them into this world so do your share to be a good role model. To all those who actually can't cook, clean or look after themselves (life skills), remember life skills are vital and should be learnt before you plan any wedding bells! Not to mention, have children. This should be avoided until you are willing to give up a lot of your own hobbies, social life, career and travel plans, etc.

No one should be selfish when it comes to pulling their weight around the home, allow the women not to be responsible for everything maybe there are some men out there that can actually do their share. My mum used to say, 'It doesn't matter if you're a man or a women, everyone gets hungry.' We all have similar needs and shouldn't expect anyone else to be responsible to do our chores for us as grown adults.

Nothing worse than feeling disrespected for expecting others do their share, if anything proper respect, love and care is not about gifts, dining out and occasionally helping, it is more about all the little things that one does every day, that shows how much a person really cares.

It is totally unfair to think that one person, usually the women can take care of all the jobs around the house. My mum used to say, 'All the jobs that a women does in the home, don't get counted" and "everyone can do one job outside of the home," what about all the different things it takes to run a home smoothly.

Never stop believing in yourself, your dreams and your goals. Everything is possible with the right mindset. That's why focussing on your own self care is vital, as focussing on every other aspects of your daily life. It is easy to get caught up in the busyness of daily life. If you are a women reading this, we tend to put everyone else's happiness, wants and needs way above our own. Then find ourselves completely drained out.

No one deserves to have all the household, family, children, chores and all the runaround being put on them solo. As my mother used to say many hands make a lighter load, if we're all able to create the mess surely we can help to clear it up too, and show their responsibility to help in all areas.

> **66**
> *PROBLEMS WILL COME IN LIFE BUT HOW WE DEAL WITH THEM IS THE SOLUTION.*
> **99**

Many years ago, when I was at high school I was always targeted by a group of Asian girls, who would call me mixed race (half cast back then) due to my slightly fairer complexion. Then after it moved onto the comments I was not able to be in their "Pepsi Posse" if I didn't do as they said. The things they asked were clearly not right, to bring in alcohol from home in a small Pepsi bottle!!! Well that wasn't going to happen, as I knew it wasn't the right thing.

I recall not telling anyone about this for a while, then the only person I did tell was my mum. Who explained how we can get caught up with the wrong people and end up getting into a routine of wrong doings, as we become like the people we spend time with. We become like the five people we hang around with the most.

Remember the people we associate ourselves with either make us or break our dreams, don't let anyone dull your sparkle. Follow that path even when it may seem like a hard lonely one.

We all have the willpower to make decisions based on ourselves, we should all be aware of allowing ourselves to become trapped in living to please others and becoming part of bad habits just to feel accepted by others. Wrong is wrong.

Sometimes being alone is harder than following the crowd, but it takes more strength to stand up for the right path and avoiding the so called peer pressure, it is easier to do wrong for most people, however I would stand my ground firmly and avoid becoming a victim to such people. Yes I know some of you will be thinking this is easier said than done, but I faced several issues of not fitting in, simply because I refused to do what I knew would be wrong and so against all that I was raised to believe and taught by my mum.

One of the most powerful parts of the human body is the mind, conquer the mind and you can conquer the world.

Remember you become like the five people you hang around with the most, choose them wisely.

> **OVERTHINKING WILL DESTROY YOUR HAPPINESS AND YOUR MOOD.**

I often get asked where I learnt to cook so well and asked to write down all my recipes up, as she was the most amazing cook ever. The truth is I was taught to cook the Indian way by my mum, freehanded... 'use your judgement", no recipe books, cards or measurements usually. Yet I cook to point today often without tasting the food, as I'm a vegetarian but often get praised for my non veg dishes by my own daughter and many others.

I wouldn't cope without my mum's recipes, all stored in my head. I would like to say however that all the base for most Indian curries is the same.

The amount of cooking and tips, I learnt from my mum was amazing and is so important.

Everyone should be doing their share, my mum use to say everyone can make the mess therefore everything should be help to tidy it. It isn't fair to expect only certain people or an individual to take responsibility of the whole household. All relationships are about compromising and shouldn't be about putting too much pressure on one person.

Moral of the story is, there is no excuse for laziness. This is not good for anyone's mental health or well-being, if they are not getting the help and support.

Common sense isn't that common anymore. If it is important we make time, if it isn't we make up excuses.

If you're like me and like to get things done, keep organised and like a clean home, chances are you will be happy with what most people may call boring or simple life. Having a roof over my and my families head, food to eat, a job and money to buy the essentials and a clean home is perfect.

Instead of complaining about bills and expenses we should all practice gratitude towards the services we are provided with and thank all the people who help deliver this to us and more. My mum was always telling us to be grateful for all that we have and she would say, money will always come and go, be thankful.

No one should be getting into a marriage until they can look after themselves. Good housekeeping number 1. It is funny that most couples have a big check list nowadays.

My mum use to say even a dog waddles its tail before it sits down. She would always say it doesn't matter if you're a boy or a girl we all get hungry, we all have a daily needs to be able to survive, therefore we must all have life skills.

> **A MOTHER IS SHE WHO CAN TAKE THE PLACE OF OTHERS BUT NO ONE CAN TAKE HER PLACE.**

Happy marriages only exist when both people work at it together and support each other equally. It is only fair that both are allowed to continue to live their life as best they can and with the women being allowed to get the help, so she can pursue her dreams and really do it all. My mum used to tell me that a lot of people don't like to see a good thing and they create lots of stories and scenarios to destroy what they don't have.

It is quite common for individuals to have a check list these days which is probably a good idea. Only if they all be honest! There is lots of cultural pressures on individuals and nothing worse than losing yourself, simply because others are raised and have different views on women. My mum use to say if you haven't raised a girl, you don't know what it is like to raise one and give her away.

In my case I was mistreated by my in laws from day one and wasn't allowed to pursue my plans, but that's another long story and a very delicate one. Luckily I moved out of their household.

I didn't tell my mum all the painful things I went through and she would ask me if I was okay and I use say yes but she would say, "I'm your mum and I know things if you tell me or not," and she would say when you become a mother you will know the feeling. She was so right.

Most men say the women moan, but in all fairness if they are left to do it all themselves and get drained out before anyone notices, it should be no surprise. Often many men who cheat blame their partner but they fail to look at their own faults. It takes a lot to run a household. My mum use to say everyone can do one job try doing the multiple tasks a women does and she would say these tasks, chores never gets counted. If you're a lazy man reading this please take responsibility for your share.

As an Indian woman myself, I can truly say the pressures I felt from in-laws after I got married were not pleasant to say the least, I was expected to put a stop to all my plans and dreams. Never lose yourself to please others, never look at someone else to love you, you must first begin with self-love, no one will truly appreciate, love or be loyal to you as you need to be to yourself. Far too much pressure is put on individuals today.

Be careful you don't allow social media to get you into a routine of what is perfection, what you see is real, be mindful of how you are driven towards expectations. Having high expectations on ourselves, is fine but remember every day, every step, effort, is getting you closer to your achievements. Don't set your standards so high that you forget to praise the little steps you achieve daily.

Everything is possible with the right mindset, dream, believe and achieve. You will have a direct impact on your health, if you can see the sights of what is causing you stress, worry or concern. Your mind is not you, your mind is very powerful and you must learn to fully utilise its abilities. Start every day with a positive mindset, you align your thoughts and actions with your highest good and best self. You will be manifesting your thoughts, so keep them positive.

Allow yourself to remove yourself from situations that are not bringing you peace. Stress can be caused because of so many factors in life, often people have several issues in themselves and no desire to identify their faults or want to seek help, but prefer to blame it on others, those who do wrong over and over should be looking at their own faults before discussing others. Don't do wrong but do what is right for you. Remember we can't control the actions of others, only how you react to the behaviour of others.

My mum use to say people are too busy looking over the fence at other people that they can't see their own faults. The stories that live inside their heads are not the truth so leave them to it.

" *'YOU CAN'T RECYCLE WASTED TIME'.* **"**

We would all benefit from connecting with our self more, self-care, self-love, self-acceptance. I strongly recommend everyone gets comfortable with doing things for themselves in their own company, without any phone and social media interruptions. It seems people are so scared to be alone with their thoughts. Our thoughts are a key to our subconscious awareness.

Taking time out to actually listen to your own thoughts, allowing the feelings to be awakened and actually connecting with yourself. Don't expect anyone to love you like you should be loving yourself. You should praise, love, support and encourage the person who looks right back at you in the mirror. Self-love is vital, connecting to your mind, body and soul is your path to happiness.

The less you focus on other people the better you will feel, their opinions are not who you are. Not everyone in our life is good for us, we must question ourselves and the company we keep. Ask yourself, if the people in your life are good for you? Do they actually want the best for you? Do they contribute to your life in a positive way?

Often we put our own happiness and feelings on hold and feel we may attend that function we don't feel comfortable with, just to show our presence, but we must not put ourselves into situations where our gut feeling doesn't feel it is the right decision.

Everything happens for a reason and we should learn from the experience.Yes I know life can feel so hard sometimes but we must first fully see our essence and take ownership of our life. Think of how our minds are more relaxed when we are resting, does your mind wonder, as we relax our minds often wonder and it is then when we are subconscious that our minds start to flow in many different directions. If we could only remove the negative distractions during the day we would, we could benefit from connecting with ourselves more.

My mum used to say we will never please them all, so we must keep our heart happy. People who want to criticise will do so regardless. One of the biggest problems in the Indian society is "what will people say" mentally, which should be replaced "who cares what people say".

We must all learn to show gratitude in all that we have and all that we are blessed with daily, your life shouldn't be a competition with anyone else, praise yourself for all that you do and your uniqueness is what shapes our world. Until it is your turn keep applauding the success of others. My mum used to say be happy for others and god is happy too, she would always tell us to be grateful every day, all day for all that we have, she would say be grateful to god for a roof over your head and food to eat. This encouraged me to do this to this day and I'm the same with my kids.

> **TIME IS VERY PRECIOUS AND REMEMBER SO ARE YOU.**

Look around at the people in your life, the things going on in your life. Make a list if it helps you to identify them, see what is good for you and brings you happiness, look at the things or people that are toxic, what are your plans to change these, you must take responsibility of all aspects of life. This is your life don't give someone else the pen to write your story.

In a world where so much information is available, we must be able to filter out the areas that are not good for our own well-being. When we get that "gut feeling" believe it, it's the energy we feel from our unconscious mind and nature has a very special way of connecting our feelings with our thoughts.

Everything will happen when it is written in your destiny and trust the universe. Know how to deal with the good, bad and the damn right ugly. Keep people in your life that bring you joy, keep you happy, keep things realistic. The ones who genuinely care, as you care about for them and your own self-care. Choose people very wisely, enjoy your own space and be strong enough to say no to people, who don't make your soul happy.

Self-respect is very important and we must not ignore our own needs, after all like my mum use to say "if we don't look after ourselves who will look after us". We can't look after anyone if we have drained ourselves out. Self-care is choosing not to argue with people who are committed to misunderstanding you.

Why do we allow our lives to be dictated so much by others, others who don't actually care for the best for us? Why do we put so much expectations on ourselves by the opinions of others? Others are not you and you are an individual, in your own right. We don't all do things, eat the same time as a baby so who puts so much pressure on us to do things by a certain age as we get older? It is all constructed in a system within society, cultures and religions but we shouldn't forget we are all individuals and unique in our rightful ways.

It seems to all so many times I've heard people say 'what will people say in the Indian culture' my reply now is who cares what they say if they don't even care about you.

We should flourish on our own paths and do what is right for us to be happy, stress free and at peace with ourselves. Nobody has it easy and we never know what people are going through, we all should think before judging, mocking or criticising. In a world where we can be anything, please be kind. Life has enough sadness we have to deal with that is beyond our control.

You should choose what is right for you, life isn't about attachments, assets, people. It all starts with you, as an individual. Don't settle for what you think will do, no one will be as honest to you as you should be to yourself. Don't be afraid to challenge your fears, don't let anyone tell you are not capable of anything, if your heart is telling something else, always listen to your inner voice. You are amazing and you are doing fantastic, you are one brave person.

As my mum used to say to me all the time, if you don't look after yourself, who is going to look after you? Only if you look after yourself will you be able to look after your children and other aspects of your life.

" SELF CARE IS A MUST CARE. "

Positive energy is felt from within and we must always try to keep our thoughts positive, hopes high, have gratitude always, rest well, feed our minds and body good, as much as we can. Live with hope in your heart, be brave and believe in yourself and your hopes.

Yoga comes from India many, many years ago. Indian head massage was a regular thing my mum did for me, as well as make all those comfort home remedies for me and the best chai.

When something makes you angry
ask yourself is it worth wasting your
energy, your precious time being angry?
Time is a very special gift. My mum use
to say silence is worth more for your
own peace.

Try to get into a routine of doing some form of meditation to relax, that can be a yoga class, pilates or even deep breathing to promote good well-being for our mindfulness. I know my mum used to pray a lot and had a very strong faith, research has proven this helps our mental well-being.

Peace is the best choice for your inner voice, you are strong enough to overcome whatever life puts you through. It's okay to make mistakes, you will find solutions as long as you don't get into a habit of making the same mistakes over and over again. Trust yourself and walk away from concerns we cannot control, believe you can change any situation that is causing you stress, learn to focus on your breathing and take timeout for a few minutes during your day, your mind will feel calmer, more relaxed and better focussed for you, just by simply taking control and connecting with your breathe is a great way to start your journey to mindfulness.

Stop thinking and start doing, we all start somewhere, if everyone didn't make that move, everyone would be stuck, then years later regret why they didn't just make a start somewhere! Do it now and do it for you. Whatever you are not happy with change it, whatever you want to achieve start now, write a list, make a plan or even some notes, just start to do something towards your dreams and believe you can do it one step at a time and it is 100% possible.

You deserve it so you're going to do better for yourself first. Sometimes people may forget how blessed they truly are. Most of you may not realise you have the key to your own destiny, every day is your chance to make that breakthrough. Your happiness doesn't live within others. Most decisions need to be made to enable us to go chase our dreams and never doubt yourself and your abilities. You must be your biggest believer.

> **EVEN THE NICEST OF PEOPLE HAVE THEIR LIMITS**

The sooner we realise that there's no such thing was the prefect weight, looks, hair or appearance for all the better, we must be proud of who we are naturally, embrace yourself and don't put added pressure on yourself to look, weight, dress etc., a certain way just to fit in anyway, either they accept you the way you are or they don't.

My mum used to say if we all were the same the world won't be the same. Be happy, be confident, be strong, be proud, be grateful and above all be yourself. Don't allow pressures from around you absorb who and what you truly are, being honest to yourself is not a weakness.

The most loyal people in this world are those who defend your name when you are not around and cheer you all the way, they are rare and the right sort of people to have in your life. My mum used to say, "People are like not being able to trust your right hand to your left hand these days," meaning those we think are close actually might not be.

I don't think having too many friends isn't always the answer personally, but having the right people in your circle is better, quality over quantity always.

It is okay to be alone and happy then to be with people who make you feel so alone, enjoy your own company, enjoy your own space, eat alone, sleep alone , dream alone and achieve alone. Silence is powerful and don't feel you must broadcast your plans to prove you are working hard, success is better done privately away from the evil eye of others, known as Naaza in Punjabi. As my mum use to tell me "not everyone has the same good heart as you and not everyone will be happy for your happiness, if you are happy for others, you too get more growth & success', she would say.

If anything is to be learnt from all this is that things we may all start to take for granted we shouldn't, someone somewhere may be praying for things so many take for granted and the universe is very powerful and can change everything at a click of a finger, as my mum used to tell me.

Practice living life with gratitude always, look in the good everywhere and in a world where you can be anything be kind. Kindness costs nothing but can be everything and make or break a person's heart.

> **" REMEMBER EVERYDAY YOU GET UP IS ANOTHER OPPORTUNITY, IT'S A GIFT SO MAKE IT COUNT. "**

Covid-19 has caused the world to shake, to rethink, recreate, replan, wait, think and think about our health, lifestyle, jobs, family and put a stop to so many things people may have all started to take for granted. Many have felt scared of not knowing what's going on, many scared of being at home, many wishing they had homeland many working endlessly to keep their homes. Sadly many lives were lost all around the globe.

It has been an eye opener for so many in many ways, some have mellowed down, some are as cruel as ever. Self-acceptance is so important, life will become easier when you accept what is. We never lose people who truly respect you, if you do it is actually a gain not a loss.

One thing is true that nothing is guaranteed, all we have is the present time. Enjoy and plan your life so you can live it to the fullest, write a to-do list is a way to physically see things and the satisfaction on ticking things off is so rewarding! Don't tell me I'm alone on this one.

Get yourself a bucket list of things you want to achieve during your life and start to work towards that. Every day is your opportunity to create wonderful things in life, it's not about a big leap, and every little step is stepping into the future, so step wisely, but keep moving into the right direction. Stop complaining about why you can't do certain things and start looking at ways to make things happen for you.

Think of what is right or wrong in your eyes at the moment, write a list of plans and work towards those goals daily before you find years have gone by yet you have not even looked or completed anything on it. Do what makes you truly happy. Love yourself more than loving the idea of other people loving you. Self-love is vital, it all starts with acceptance and appreciating ourselves.

Don't fall back into old patterns because you feel okay there. Go live your life to the fullest. Enjoy the little things as they are the things that are important as well, before it's too late, then you realise they were actually the big things.

Having the right mentality and motivation is important to getting on with simple daily life, avoid distractions, bad energy, poor concentration and feeling the pressure of being like others. You are unique and you should embrace that. More green time and less screen time.

There seems to be far too much screen time distractions these days, my mum used to say 'The tv will never say stop watching me and go do some work', this is even more powerful today with all the mobile devices, social media and gaming around. This is also a very bad habit, can become addictive and reduce your energy levels. Remember everything you see online isn't the real deal.

> **"**
> *THE BEST REVENGE IS NO REVENGE, MOVE ON AND BE HAPPY.*
> **"**

Always try to remember the three C's in life, choices, chances and changes. Value yourself for who you actually are, don't allow others to dictate your worth. Trust yourself, think for yourself. Have your own opinions and stand by your choices.

If you get the chances take the right ones, don't underestimate which chance is to be taken and which ones should be avoided for you. Only you have the power to change what you are not happy with in life, don't be afraid of change, embrace it, live it and blossom through it all.

I always say if it won't evolve me, please don't involve me. If it feels wrong, it most probably is wrong for you.

We may cross paths with certain people who instantly makes us feel calm, refreshed, alive and whole. We may feel as if we have known them for a long time just because the communication is at a better level, the vibes are good and the energy feels right. The ones who encourage you to follow your dreams and celebrate your wins without a bit of jealously.

They want the best for you, even if you aren't sure of what that is yourself, you also want the best for them. There is not usually much more to it or this one person can be your whole world. They are warm and bright, loving, caring, loyal and very intelligent. You can't help feeling so safe, secure and happy in their presence, like the best version of yourself. For me that special person was my beautiful amazing mum.

As my beautiful mum is no longer with me, I keep her memories alive as much as I can, not a single day or hour goes by without me thinking of her. All the things I learnt from her has shaped me to the women I am today. Bereavement is hard, it is very hard especially if you had a close, open, honest and loving relationship.

Those who knew my mum were blessed with her pure heart and soul, she was the most loveable person ever, some appreciated this, some didn't. No matter how cruel life was to get she was still the nicest person I knew. Many would comment on her little quotes and sayings, most of which I use often myself.

If you ever find yourself in situations that actually drain you, don't feel afraid to say no and remove yourself from that situation. My mum would tell me "you will never please them all, so start by pleasing yourself and stop draining yourself out for people who wouldn't even notice." I prefer to keep my energy and vibes positive and do things that make me happy.

Recognise your potential don't allow others to criticise you, keep your focus in mind and if possible avoid sharing everything with others too easy. Keep your circle small and most importantly keep it real.

> **IT'S NOT AGE THAT MAKES YOU MATURE, IT'S RESPONSIBILITIES.**

Believe you are capable, you are worthy and you are able to achieve your dreams.

Remind yourself it is okay to say no to invites you don't feel like attending, it's okay to hide away and spend quality time on yourself and your well-being. Never force yourself to do things that are causing you more pain and discomfort, this is your time and your life. No one should feel they have to keep putting the happiness of others before their own inner peace.

Too many people think about what other people would say, when most the so called other people wouldn't even careless about you anyway. They are not the people who walk in your shoes every day, they are not living your life and they don't even know your full story, they may base it on the chapter they walked in on. Do not allow the opinion of those who do so little for you take up so much of your precious time.

Be so positive that negative people don't want to be near you. I prefer to keep my personal life simply "personal". I am not a huge fan of sharing everything with everyone and I don't trust people too easily. I'm actually a happy soul being in my own space, please don't misunderstand me but I like the simple things in life, I am happy with just the basic simple things in life and having the gratitude with a happy heart. I have overheard so many conversations like "he said', 'she said/did' that no one will actually know the truth of anything but the individual who the subject is about.

We spent so much of our time working, but we mustn't forget to find our passion and purpose in life. Don't get caught up in making a living that you forget to make the most of your life. If it doesn't bring you joy it isn't your path. Create an income from what you love not from what you see others doing.

My mum used to say, we have to be in the children's presence to be in their future. Give them the gift of your presence not the gifts money buys. The bond is only strong if you build a connection. Your time is the most valuable asset, spend it wisely. I think most mums tend to put so much pressure and guilt on ourselves. No matter what we do we tend to get criticised regardless, so do what feels right for your heart and is best for your child(ren).

During the school run I overheard a child ask her mother 'Why do you have to go to work mummy," she replied "so we can have nice things.' Us mums feel guilty if were stay at home, go to work, overworking, underworking, cook meals at home from scratch, cook a ready meal, go out solo or do anything for self-care, etc. We are all guilty of letting ourselves feel over pressured of what is right or wrong.

We have to go with our mother's instincts, yes we mums have a superpower!

> **SOMETIMES WHAT DIDN'T WORK OUT FOR YOU ACTUALLY WORKED OUT PERFECTLY TO BRING YOU WHERE YOU ARE DESTINED TO BE.**

Somedays everything may seem 'Overwhelming and impossible, take a deep breathe or two, pause and remind yourself you will get through wherever life takes you too, just learn how to deal with all the things and reward yourself for getting there.

Believe you are so close to getting everything you have been working for. Feel it in your soul and believe it is your time and you are ready now. We are all here with a purpose, we all have our own plans for our life. Avoid distractions and being around negative people. Keep your vibes positive and thoughts happy. As my mum used to teach me, always turn the negatives into positives and you will see how blessed you truly are.

You may not always take the time out to see or feel like it sometimes, but you could see yourself through the eyes of someone who loves you will, then you would see how amazing you are…Yes you are …You got this.

If like me the pandemic has made you realise who is actually there for you and who I would like to stay away from. One thing is for sure, we must not look for someone else to make us happy, we must be happy with ourselves. Happiness starts with yourself, never give the key to your happiness to anyone else. It's up to you to give yourself the self-love you desire.

How others react to your sparkle isn't your problem, never let anyone dull your sparkle. Dream as big as you want but believe as big as you dream, don't let small minded people tell you, you can't achieve it. People who feel they need to control others, don't have control over themselves. My mum used to say "A thief sees everyone as a thief." Often people who are guilty themselves see everyone else guilty too.

Don't be afraid of losing people, be afraid of losing yourself by trying to please everyone else. Sometimes happiness is staying at home, saying no to others, minding your own business and putting yourself first. Dream it, believe it and achieve it.

Instead of attaching yourself to the TV, social media, emails or mobile encourage yourself to get into a good routine to mediate, pray or take a walk in nature, this will promote better energy and relaxation. We can't avoid stress but we can learn how to manage it. Psychology says stress is not all bad for us if only we know how to address it and know how to manage it, we can use it to send better positive signals to our brains.

Removing distractions is vital if you want to accomplish more. Make the sacrifices now to build a better future.

> *I HATE WHEN PEOPLE'S WORDS DON'T MATCH THEIR ACTIONS AFTER ALL ACTIONS DO SPEAK LOUDER THAN WORDS.*

The power of sleep is highly underestimated in today's society, we build while we sleep, getting into a routine for bedtime is just as important for an adult as it is for a child. Not only does it give us our energy but it helps us be more proactive.

My mum use to tell me early morning dreams are always true, this has helped me so much as I have dreamt of her so many times and the early morning ones have answered so many of my unanswered questions, since her passing.

Realise you are perfect in your own unique way and you should be proud of the person you are, who you can be and what you are becoming, beyond the thought of an image you put so much pressure on yourself about life. You are enough, imagine your life in several years from now, imagine not being sat and thinking of your life and how you never wore that bikini as you felt your body wasn't "perfect" for the beach because of what you imagined is perfect and told yourself what is right and wrong.

Imagine not doing all the things you wanted to but didn't make time for yourself, you didn't say no to the things you would rather not do, instead you put extra pressure on yourself of what is perfect and looks about perception consumed you from many forms, than finally realising you covered yourself up to avoid showing your scars, stretch marks, etc.

You avoided so many things you wanted to do but had an image in your mind of what is perfect so missed out on living and being true to yourself for the sake of others, all the years you have wasted hating yourself, but now it is too late as you no longer have the ability to. Remember live life now and you are enough and always have been, embrace your uniqueness. My mum used to say 'If we all looked the same the world, the world wouldn't be as colourful" . Be enough for yourself first and the rest of the world can wait.

We all have seen better days but we have seen worse ones too. We may not have everything that we want but we have all that we need. You may have woken up with some aches and pains but at least you woke up, life may not be perfect but remember you are blessed. What you may take for granted someone, somewhere may be praying for. Always count your blessings all the time and with a grateful heart is the key to happiness.

It doesn't matter how slow you go as long as you don't stop for too long, as you are work in progress, like we all are.

66

ENJOY THE LITTLE THINGS IN LIFE, KEEP IT SIMPLE

99

It is okay not be invited, included or considered by others, just don't do that to your own peace of mind. Accept it is what it is and move on for your own inner peace. The quality of your life is a direct reflection of the quality of your thoughts, beliefs and daily habits. Remember we can't be responsible for the behaviour of others. The world can feel like a cold place sometimes but don't let this affect your loving warm heart.

The only person you should be working to improve is the person you were yesterday, keep improving yourself for yourself. Don't think you can't achieve anything you want, just because other people have already done things quicker than you, doesn't mean you can't get things done. It is all about timing, when it's right it will happen for you.

Don't feel you need to put so much pressure on yourself and remember our lives are our unique chapters. Just like our births, we aren't all born on the same day, at the same place, time, we are all capable of achieving what we dream about in live with hard work and determination. Don't feel you need to tell everyone your plans, after all believing starts with you, you are going to be your biggest believer.

Trust the universe and never lose that goal you have in mind. It will all happen for the best but never lose that faith and keep believing. Focus on your own road and take control of the map, this is your life and your journey, the journey of life.

Mums hold our hands for a short time but our hearts forever, the strength, encouragement and support I had from my mum is irreplaceable. The knowledge she has passed onto me I honour and share with so many, in hope it will inspire so many beautiful souls.

It is often said that robins appear when your angels are near, my garden is often full of robins and their nests, find the little comforts that remind you that our loved ones are never too far. From dreams that get your unanswered questions answered, to places, scents, taste, items, locations, colours all bring sentimental feelings and fond memories that take you to your comfort zone.

> **" DON'T SHARE EVERYTHING WITH EVERYONE, YOUR SUCCESS WILL SPEAK FOR ITSELF. DON'T LET THE DOUBTERS MAKE YOU DOUBT YOURSELF. "**

Respect yourself enough to walk away from anything that doesn't give you peace. Don't let the behaviour, words or actions of others put you down. It is often said 'hurt people, hurt people", remind yourself not everyone deserves or will appreciate your good heart, that's okay, just don't think two wrongs will make a right. Never hurt those who hurt you, instead forgive them for your own peace.

Don't let the bitterness of others ruin the good soul you are. Never feel you need to apologise for anything that means you're putting yourself first, even though as mums we know this is highly unlikely, if you are a hands on mum who is so proud to put her children first. Remember if you don't look after your own well-being don't expect anyone else to notice either. You will be struggling to look after anyone if you don't look after yourself.

When you learn that a person's behaviour has more to do with their own internal struggle than it ever did with you, you will learn we can't take control of their actions, decisions or behaviours. We can only control how we chose to react to it.

We can't help anyone if they don't thing they need the help first and can't see anything wrong with their behaviour. My mum use to say so many people suffer and instead of becoming better humans they continue to hurt others, instead of doing good deeds they continue to be bitter, jealous and angry. She would say an angry person only ruins their own face by frowning.

Self-love should be a daily routine to ourselves. We must embrace ourselves, so we can prioritise our own mental well-being, as well as physical and spiritual. Your life is all about the decisions you make. Once you start to love yourself it doesn't matter who doesn't love you. Believe in yourself, self-worth is worth more than other people's value of you. Instead of loving the idea of someone else loving you learn to love yourself unconditionally.

Enjoy your own company, I love my own company even more so since the pandemic. I like the peace, silence, no distractions of modern life gadgets, the distance from certain people, the calm within my own space. Too many people are afraid to be alone and would rather be with the wrong company, too many people can't see the true friends to those that come disguised. Some people will never like you because your good spirit irritates their fake souls.

Everyone we meet isn't meant to continue the whole journey of life with you. Everything happens for a reason.

> " BLOOD MAY MAKE YOU RELATED
> BUT LOYALTY MAKES YOU
> FAMILY. "

When you set boundaries it is to attempt to make a safe space for your own mindfulness. Remember not everyone you meet is meant to continue the whole journey of life with you. Be around people who respect and appreciate you, the ones who understand it's a privilege to be in your life, the ones who have your back no matter what and not only when it suits their needs of you, the ones who are happy for your happiness. The ones who feel your pain, the people who cheer for your achievements. The people who are truly 100% honest, loyal, loving, caring, thoughtful, appreciative and always genuine.

It is okay to remove yourself and disconnect with anyone who doesn't feel right for your own well-being. It is better not to have people in your life who make you feel invisible and only remember you when they need you. Never forget who was there for you when you were at your lowest point and who was there for you in your happy times.

Friends and family doesn't mean nothing if they aren't making a positive impact on your life. Toxic is toxic, related or not. Most energies come disguised as friends and family.

If the favours would never be returned, think before you put yourself forward. Always make time for the things and people that make you happy and are good for your soul. Learn from the past, embrace the present and believe in the future. Remember nothing lasts forever.

Don't ignore your own thoughts and feelings. Avoid turning to comfort eating, social media or any other bad habit, often these actions are done to avoid dealing with the real issues that are annoying us. Only you can help heal yourself. Walking in nature outdoors is good for the mind.

Make every day as amazing as you can, see the good in all. The word 'impossible' actually can spell 'I'm possible', a positive mindset will help your growth, thinking and your beliefs. Be the best version of yourself, love yourself and be compassionate, share your kindness with others. Do it for yourself, no one matters as much as you do to yourself. Self-care should be a priority and not just something we do time to time, after let downs or disappointments.

One thing I have learnt the hard way is, that no matter how much I do for others they won't actually bother to make me a priority. This world seems to be all about the need of others and it does hurt when we realise just because we made time for others, it doesn't mean they will make time for us in the same way. My mum use to say the world is only about their needs.

> **THERE COMES A TIME WHEN YOU HAVE TO STOP CROSSING OCEANS FOR PEOPLE WHO WOULDN'T EVEN JUMP PUDDLES FOR YOU**

It is best to think of your own happiness and well-being before you put yourself out for anyone, unless of course they are the rare few who are always there for you too. If you have these people or person in your life, cherish them as they are very rare and unique. But don't drain yourself out pleasing the ungrateful.

Accept you're not for everyone, accept you are unique and you have standards. My mum used to say if people are going to talk about you they will, regardless if it's good or bad, they just got to talk! Let them make up their own versions. You just got to know what should be addressed and what should be ignored. Just be yourself and don't let anyone dull your sparkle.

In today's society things are very different, I remember the lovely memories of having a busy household at my mum's house, where the doors were always open to guests coming and going on the weekends. My mum was always prepared for any unexpected guests and I remember the atmosphere was always so happy and welcoming.

My mum used to say in years to come no one will go to anyone's without an invitation, those were the good old days for sure. Nowadays it all becoming a competitive world, people are becoming more obsessed with strangers online than actually focussing on real people, sharing kindness, helping each other, showing gratitude and being grateful. People are complaining about lack of time but fail to see all the distractions that are taking up their time, time they could be using in a more productive way.

I tend to avoid people and places I don't feel welcomed for comfortable around now, if there's a bad vibe it isn't worth my time! Be that strong person, let them think it is a bad attitude, it is having boundaries they don't like. Having boundaries is good and shouldn't be broken to please others. Don't put yourself into situations where you feel so uncomfortable and unhappy, your inner peace, mental wellbeing is far more important than anything else.

Be careful what you and others put out there into the world, in a world where you can be anything, be kind. One harsh act could be enough to push anyone to the end. No one wants anyone to treat them horribly and no one should feel bullied into accepting cruel behaviour from others.

Those who truly love you will allow you to fully blossom, live the life you dream and support you to achieve them and be there for you no matter what. Most bullies usually play victim and are happy to twist the truth and believe the lies they keep inside their own head to maintain a fake image to others. Like my mum use to say to me when we deal with such people, 'You can cover the eyes of people but you can't cover the eyes of god.'

> **" DON'T BE AFRAID OF LOSING PEOPLE BE AFRAID OF LOSING YOURSELF BY TRYING TO PLEASE EVERYONE AROUND YOU. "**

We can't control the behaviour of others but we can control how we react, what we allow, accept and forgive. It if costs you, your peace it's not worth it. If they care they make the time, if they don't they make up excuses. If they don't involve you, don't get involved, if they don't tell you don't bother to ask, if they don't remember you don't bother to remind them, if they don't ask for your opinion don't give it, your gut instincts will tell you, listen to the signs.

Your time and energy is precious, use it wisely and put yourself and your peace of mind first. Don't worry what people say behind your back, they are behind you for a reason, if they aren't real enough to say it to your face, they aren't worth it. I've learnt people will make up stories about you so they can look like a better person, it is fine at least they took time out to create something in their life to make me a priority! The truth always comes out in the end.

Happy Mind Happy Life, the world is your oyster! Maturity is in the mind and not age.

When you give others your time they assume you are always free, the truth is you make time for what is important, value the time. In a world that seems to be full of dishonest people, honest people can come across as hurtful, some people don't like to hear the truth and like the saying goes, the truth always hurts.

You are far more than your physical appearance, my mum use to always say, a good person is one who has a clean heart, clear conscience. Let your soul be right from within, it is not all about being perfect on the outside, true beauty starts from within. Look after your soul so your soul can look after you.

I know life's not always sweet like chocolate but if things get bitter, remember you can handle anything with a strong positive mindset. Never stop being a good person because of bad people. Don't allow the behaviour of others ruin your inner calm.

The truth always comes out in the end so don't worry what the toxic people are saying or doing to hurt you, as my mum used to say to me, the more happy you remain the more they burn.

I am such a firm believer in gut instincts, as I've aged I'm less of a people pleaser and look out for those who look out for me and my children. Those who are transparent, kind and joyful to be around. Don't get me wrong, we all go through times when our thoughts, emotions and scenery aren't that we would hope for but it is all temporary. We cannot afford to waste our time trying to please others, when others don't appreciate our presence, contribution and honesty. My mum used to say, life is such a precious gift.

> **"**
> *DON'T SAY WHY ME, SAY TRY ME,*
> *YOU GOT THIS!*
> **"**

Our time is very precious and none of us know exactly how much time we have, don't waste it dwelling on the things we can't change, we just need to accept it or change it. If it is something beyond our control we just accept it and move on.

Even the eyes can be misleading as no one can see inside another person's soul. Don't let others ruin the kind person you are. There will always be people who don't actually know you but hate their own version of you, let them be. Your energy isn't to be wasted on such people. Your purpose is much bigger than anyone's version of you. Keep your goals to yourself and don't share everything with everyone, negative energy can make you lose your focus.

Not everyone has the heart to smile and cheer on someone else's happiness, success or goals. Nothing makes me happier than seeing others happy, living a happy fulfilled life, it is the little things that count as well.

It is good to have your dreams, plan, goals, ambitions and desires, just be careful who you share them with. Let the success speak for itself, be grateful and stay humble. Always help those less fortunate than yourself and never look down on anyone, unless you are helping them up. The way someone fits you into their schedule, says a lot about what they think of you, always remember that.

Never forget the one person who you have probably had more conversations with than anyone else, the one person who will never leave you, that person is very important, they have helped you before anyone else and will be with you until your last breath, that person is so precious and that person is you.

Don't let others define what you can or can't do, make time to relax, remember it is okay to do nothing if your body is telling you to just chill and read a book, watch something listen to that music to uplift your moods. Don't let others tell you that you can't have fun without doing certain things or taking certain things, like alcohol, partying or socialising. Nothing wrong with doing what you feel is right for you in your own space to relax.

With all the stress and strains of modern lifestyle, social media and the pressures that come from society, it is important to be able to identify what makes you happy, relaxed, at peace and what doesn't. Accept it is okay to say no, don't be afraid to lose people for putting your well-being first. Remember we never lose the right people, we learn how to remove the toxic ones.

"

LIVE AND LET LIVE.

"

No matter how near or far you are from someone who truly cares for you, they will be there for you no matter what the time of day. True friendships aren't based on who has been there the longest but who has remained loyal, through the good, the bad and the damn right ugly situations. Everyone can be there for you during the good times but the real ones are the ones who are there for you throughout the ups and downs of life, they are your real cheerleaders.

If you have good people around you cherish them, cherish the time you have together and create beautiful memories. The simple things are the best things, in fact it's not the things it is the people and our minds that are valuable.

It is your life and you must make it the best possible one for you, it's not going to last forever, nothing is promised, cherish every second and make it the best story for yourself. As we go through life we shouldn't look back on our life with regrets, of what we wished we had done differently, we should look back at the memories we have created for ourselves and with the people around us that are important.

Cherish the time we had, although too short in my case with my mum. I remember my mum telling me that some children don't even get to see their mothers, as many die from childbirth, that is truly heartbreaking, she used to say, no child should lose their mother.

Good people with good hearts, good intentions and loyalty are far and few but they do exist, if you can't find them be sure to be one. Two wrongs don't make a right so it's important to remain honest to yourself even when others have hurt you.

I have heard the saying that good people with good hearts are the ones who get hurt the most, but I think it is because people with good hearts have good intentions and when others aren't the same, it hurts more to a person who is caring.

In life we meet people from all walks of life, we learn a lesson for life or an experience from them. Keep hope of that you want in life and not of what you don't want. Positive mindset is the key to a positive mind. Every little bit of information you reserve or retrieve gets into our minds, we just decide what we want to absorb, store or dispose. It is all the overloading and overthinking that can disrupt our peace of mind.

Don't judge each day by the harvest that you reap but by the seeds you plant. Those who do wrong will eventually have to deal with their own karma.

Positive people can also have negative thoughts but we must learn to not allow these thoughts to take over our daily mindset, inner peace and lifestyle. We all face problems in life that we can't avoid but they are a part of life, we mustn't allow them to take over our life.

Every hurdle we cross we will become stronger, wiser and more intelligent in many ways, often unknown to ourselves until we find ourselves in similar situations and we recall how to deal with things differently, better or how to avoid crossing the same paths.

> 66
> *TO EVOLVE YOU MUST BE WILLING TO RESOLVE, STARTING WITH ANYTHING THAT IS UNHEALED FROM WITHIN.*
> 99

Ever heard the saying 'didn't your mum teach you some sense?' The fact is most mums try their best to teach their child common sense, but like my mum used to say if a person chooses not to listen and is ignorant to take pride in listening, there isn't much point in saying much more!! Often everyone learns in their own time, therefore let others make their mistakes and hopefully learn a lesson for life.

Silence is the best response to a fool, let the fools think they have fooled you. Silence is more powerful to people who are too comfortable in misunderstanding you. Remember not everyone who shakes your hand is your friend, be wise who you pick as your "friends", true friendships are rare and few. Quality over quantity always.

Life will usually test you before it blesses you. Turn up for yourself every day and praise yourself for how well you're doing. Things usually hit us very hard before we realise it isn't for us and it's time to move on. Gratitude is the best medicine.

When you hang around with all the wrong people you become like them, the problem with today's society is not many people like to be a leader, it is easier for many to follow the crowd. It is better to be alone than it is to be with the wrong crowd.

Still the same person just with a different mindset. Never underestimate the power of your thoughts. If you continue to think the way you always have, you will continue to get what you always have. Change your thoughts, change your energy, change your mindset, and focus on your positive vibes. Life begins when your fears end, allow yourself to set outside your comfort zone.

Keep working towards the dreams and remember every step you take is getting you closer. One positive thought can change your day, make sure your mind is stronger than your emotions, head over heart or you will lose yourself every time.

Do not correct a fool or they will hate you, correct a wise person they will appreciate your views.

Sometimes the only way to truly be happy is to just let go of anything that is no longer at peace with you and see what comes next. Don't stress about anything that was not in your power and let yourself heal. Overthinking won't resolve anything but it will have a negative impact on your peace of mind. When in doubt leave it out.

People are much nicer when they are happy within themselves, which says a lot about people who aren't very nice to you. Wish them well and be on your way......

Your mind is very powerful it is absorbing information from many resources, don't allow it to be overflowing with things you want to avoid. Sometimes life makes us suffer before we can shine, we don't know how strong we are until being strong is the only option. Life usually tests us before it blesses us.

> **FOLLOW YOUR HEART BUT REMEMBER TO TAKE YOUR BRAIN WITH YOU.**

My mum wasn't keen on following others, she had such a strong caring personality, naturally beautiful and was the least materialistic person I knew. She would say no matter what you wear a person's face will stay the same and if you're not a nice person with a good heart nothing will make you look beautiful. Her way of seeing true beauty is from within and having good intentions is vital.

My mum was truly one in a zillion, I learnt so much from my amazing mum, helping others, to embracing choices for myself. She was a firm believer that we are all unique and special in our own life. Many would comment and still do to this day on her beautiful soul inside and out.

She truly was, and it is because of my mum and all that I learnt from her and her teaching, quotes and sayings, that when I used to tell others, many would say I should write a book as their mum's never taught them the things I tell them. With the thoughts I have and the teaching I've learnt from my dearest mother, I hope this book brings you some inspiration too.

I believe everything is all connected to the universe and we all have our story to tell in this world. Like my mum used to say, the world is full of different types of people, we all look different and we all are as unique as the imprints on our fingerprints, but what we choose to do while we are here we should think wisely. She was a women with a heart as sure as can be, she would help everyone. She had the most grateful heart and was the most appreciative person I knew.

I am so truly grateful to God for giving me the most amazing mother.

Always in my heart until we met again.

> *A MOTHER IS SHE WHO CAN TAKE THE PLACE OF OTHERS BUT NO ONE CAN TAKE HER PLACE.*

Thank you for purchasing my book and I truly hope it gives you some inspiration.

This book is dedicated to my beautiful mother, my daughter for encouraging me to write it, all those who have told me to write a book, and last but not least to you who is reading this now.

I wish each and everyone of you the very best in life.

Regards,
Baljinder

Lightning Source UK Ltd.
Milton Keynes UK
UKHW020901080322
399734UK00006B/99

9 781915 164599